UNSEEN Scars

MARTIN TERRELL

EXPLORA BOOKS
700 – 838 West Hastings St. Vancouver, BC V6C 0A6
www.explorabooks.com
Phone: (604) 330 6795

ISBN: 978-1-998394-77-7 (Paperback)
978-1-998394-86-9 (Hardback)
978-1-998394-78-4 (eBook)

UNSEEN

Scars

MARTIN TERRELL

Contents

Chapter One

I Want To Live

Unseen Scars

There's a scar there because I can feel it,
Seems like it's been there forever,

Running like a six-lane highway
through the vortex of my soul.

"Any new scars boy?"
The officer rasped.

"None that you can see,"
I countered with a laugh.

Yes, I have some scars,
and a few of them are new.

But none are as deep and ugly
as those inflicted by you.

Calloused as an eagle's talons,
putrid scars, pus-encrusted and mean,

Seared at birth, and scarred forever,
The birthright and legacy of the unseen.

The three-inch slash beneath my beard
grows deeper and uglier each day.

A gift from a weighted nightstick
drumming a tune we both knew well.

But it's the scar inside that disfigures me,
contorts my reasoning, and smothers hope.

Bile is sweet compared to its secretion.
Hatred, despair, and submission.

Show me your scars," the officer barked,
I tilted my head back and laughed.

MYOPIA

Will I recognize Justice
When I find it?
Maybe Justice is a small town
Hidden away like the Emerald City,

Where the Wizard of Justice
Lives behind a screen
Shaking everything up and
Making lots of noise,

Keeping the game the same
And just changing its name.
Abracadabra-ing Ghettos
Into Inner Cities

Hasn't changed anything
But the description of
Poverty is still the same.
The unemployable

Are still the underclass.
Some say,
Justice is a gated community
South of Neverland

With a Club house at the 19th hole.
Nobody that I know lives there.
They couldn't get past the gate.
'Cause everybody who lives in

Justice Looks like everyone else-
And none of them look like me.
Justice's citizens keep Injustice alive
While judging the rest of us,

And keeping most of
Everything for themselves.
This proves Justice isn't really
Blind, She's just Myopic.

Some Folks Call Them Hostages

Most folks tell me there was a riot at the
White House the other day.

Others say 't was an insurrection.
A few say there was some protesting going on
And these protestors were arrested.

Having been a protestor myself,
I don't remember ever beating
A policeman during my protests.
Or destroying federal property and
Invading private offices of elected Officials.

Now, some folks tell me these protestors
Who beat policemen and destroyed
Federal property were convicted of
A number of different charges and Sent to prison.

Other folk say these folk who are now
In prison are actually hostages.

Fighters For freedom being held hostage as part
Of the struggle. What struggle? Hostages?
Black mothers say that Black men are the real hostages!

Some say that 1.8 million
Black sons, brothers, and husbands are in jail or prison today.
Sure sounds like hostages to them.

When just 13% of the general population,
Represents 37% of the prison population,

Something is amiss.
There's a war going on somewhere.
Hostages from the White House Riots,
Be for real. What war are you fighting?

Who are you fighting against?
Black mothers say: Shut yo' mouth.
You can't even spell struggle yet. But you can learn,
While you're waiting for your leader to get you out.

Ain't No Coincidence

Ain't no coincidence
That everyone in my neighborhood
Knows someone or has someone
Who has been in jail

Ain't no coincidence
That some women in my neighborhood
Have children living at home,
Don't have a job,
And are on welfare.

Ain't no coincidence
That many of the men in my neighborhood,
Are on their way to jail,
Or are on parole.

Ain't no coincidence
That black folk are historically
Restricted to living conditions,
That foster self-destructiveness.

Ain't no coincidence
Ain't no white folks
Living in my neighborhood.

Endangered Species

When are you going to stop
Crying racism, and injustice?!
When you stop enforcing injustice and murder!
What about the fairness and opportunities you see?

Opportunities to die in the street for me.
You refuse to see
That I am a Black male
And death dances all around me.

I cannot ignore the nightly news
And pundits' views announcing...
"Another Black male mistaken for a burglar,
Shot to death by four white policeman".

I am an endangered species.
My preserve, a prison.
My killing grounds, city streets.
My killers, municipal assassins.

Who will stop the ugliness?
Who will save me?
Who will put the Black Male on the
Endangered species list? The White Rhino is.

Moments in between
As long as you are riding my back,
You can squeeze,
Release and Squeeze my neck at will.

Those moments in between my choking
Feel like freedom- but they are not
For as long as you are riding my back.
My freedom is only a delusion.

True freedom cannot be found until I have broken,
Or chewed your fingers from around my neck.
And I can stand up as you can stand.
And shatter a delusion of freedom, that never was.

Rainbow Man

I am rainbow man,
Not like in Somewhere
Over The Rainbow,

'Cause ain't no bluebirds
Flying in my rainbow
Only birds flying

In my rainbow are crows,
You don't see 'em
'cause they're black.

You can't tell one thing
From the other,
In a black rainbow

Just different views
Of blackened hues
And an empty pot of gold.

Already Guilty

His whole life
He's been treated

Like he's already Guilty.
He knows that

No matter how Good he is
At survivor speak

No matter how many Yes Sirs and No Sirs,
Or how good he is at Sucking up.

He is already Guilty,
Guilty of Being Black.

Policemen say
He's dangerous,

Uses deadly force,
He's already Guilty.

They All Look the Same

When is Black America going to grow up?
When are we going to stop crying and praying
And wringing our hands?
It's disgusting to watch

The same tired script,
Echoed over and over.
They all look the same
When I turn on the TV

They all look the same Black women crying,
Screeching, Throwing their hands Up In the air
Screaming and falling down
Too weak to stand.

They all look the same
Nothing's going to change
I've seen it all before
Black men dead in The streets

Not every Black man Is a criminal
And not Every cop a Killer
But for my survival
Every cop is seen

As a Municipal Assassin
And I must live
As if it's so.
They all look the same.

It's The Car Stupid

You can prep him
Give him good manners,
"A pleasure to meet you, sir."
Give him a great education,

"Ivy League's the best, they say."
You can love him,
Build his self-confidence
Even teach him self-defense.

But don't, don't give him a car
Especially a new luxury car.
As any policeman will tell you
The only Black men

Who drive new luxury cars are Criminals-
Especially those pimps and drug dealers
With ivy-league degrees
Even a college VP looks like a drug dealer.

To a cop. Most college VP's I've known
Look more disheveled than drug dealers.
After driving a five-year-old Jag
VJ6 through a stop sign,

I stopped before the officer reached me.
He looked stonily at my car,
Ignored my white wife and toned,
"You got any warrants out for you?"

"Boy," was left hanging silently in the Air for us both to hear.
We were in Port Jefferson, New York,
Minutes from Stoney Brook, the college
Where I worked.

I kinda chuckled and shook my head; "No, sir."
He admonished me, didn't give me a ticket
And let me on my way.
Maybe if I were in a five-year-old Ford Falcon

I wouldn't have gotten stopped.
He didn't know we were a mixed couple
Until he walked up to the car-
And he didn't know

That he had just Busted
A 61-year-oldpimp or Drug dealer.
Now that was the bust of the year.
Do you think it might have been the car?

STILL A SLAVE

After the War of Northern
Aggression Northerners picked slaves up,
Dressed them in freedom,
Pen stroked them free,

Christened them as Negroes
And loosed them blindly
Upon the land.
After seeing what they had done

Northerners smiled,
And felt morally Superior to Southerners.
But Southerners Knew the Negro was
Still a slave by another name,

And continued,
To treat him as one.
Over time,
Negro slave quarters,

Became the Ghetto
And the new slave quarters
The Inner-City.
Slaves of the Inner-City

Weren't Negro, or even Black.
They were educated,
African-Americans, with a hyphen.
And still treated as slaves.

Inner-City slaves became
Slaves to their enslavement,
Unwitting victims, and Architects of their own destruction -
And Southerners smiled.

EYEWITNESS NEWS

The leading cause of
Death of Black men
Under 30 are other black men,
Studies show.

"Mess with me and
Your ass will end up
On Eyewitness
News," they vow.

Blacks are always
Killing each other,
On Eyewitness News.

Yet, they rarely kill whites -
Too dangerous where whites
To live or not-to-live in
Black neighborhoods.

Blacks are addicts,
Rapists, robbers, or thugs.
Blacks are known killers,
On Eyewitness News.

Night after night
At your dinner table
Or in your living room,
Blacks are terrifying.

If I was White and
Only knew Black men
Through Eyewitness News,

I'd cross the street
Whenever I saw a
Black Man coming toward
Me and double-lock,
My front door,
When the sun went down.

But if I lived in certain
Parts of North Carolina,
I'd shoot and kill a Black man
Whenever he came
Knocking at my door.

THE BROWN SORCERERS

They don't lynch brown men
Burn them on a cross,
Or drag them through Main St.
Tied to the back of a pickup
Truck like blacks.

They just handcuff 'em,
Behind the back,
Throw 'em in the back
Seat of a Police Car
And let 'em shoot themselves.

Brown men are very powerful
Sorcerers, policemen say.
They make guns with brown magic,
With their hands 'cuffed behind their
Backs. and then shoot themselves
In the head.

Brown sorcerers are not very wise
Shooting themselves in the head,
In the back seat of Police cars,
With their hands 'cuffed
Behind their backs.

If Brown sorcerers are really
wise, and could make
themselves guns,
while sitting in the back seat of Police
Cars with their hands 'cuffed behind
their backs,

why don't they shoot the
Policemen sitting in the front

seats, and make their getaway,
with their hands 'cuffed behind
their backs? If I were a Sorcerer
that's what I would do.

PASS THE BOOTS PLEASE

How can you pick yourself up
By your bootstraps,
When you don't have any Boots?

My neighborhood is
Littered with broken-down homes,
Broken people and vacant tots.

Where's that 40 acres
And a mule,
When I need it?

The neighborhood is a conduit,
A pass-through to go
Somewhere else.

It is in permanent transition
With transitional people
Stuck in place,

Throwaways in the projects
Warily watch would-be victims
Passing further south to the Ball Park

It is a neighborhood of streets
And numbers that makes it easier
For outsiders to define poverty,

By branding its offspring
As drug addicts
And criminals.

Those numbers are there for anyone to
see, And those of us inside the numbers
Are crippled by them.

Pass the boots,
please, if you can find them,
I'd like to pick myself up.

IT'S JUST BUSINESS

Neighborhoods are
inseparable;
From the street's numbers,
And that makes it easier to discriminate.

Cabbies know that best of all.
Cabbies know the neighborhoods
Those numbers represent.
So, they discriminate.

They choose not to go into areas
That they believe to be dangerous,
Or they have little opportunity
For making money.

They don't consider it discrimination
Against the people who live in that neighborhood.
If you ask them.
It's just good business.

THE DANGEROUS GAME

Seers, prophets, and
Messiahs play a very
Dangerous game.

Seers are often punished,
Prophets and Messiahs
Often killed.

For telling the truth
To those who don't want
Their truths exposed:

Truths exposed to others,
And truths about themselves.

Truth tellers are often blind
And need no eyes to see.

"I can see right through you,"
Said the blind subway

Seer, "Your soul is inside out."
Truth tellers often dole out
Their truths in such language.

Makes their truths easier to embrace
But more difficult to discard.

Hearing the truth
Can be as dangerous, as telling it,
And much more difficult to accept.

Truth haters believe that killing
The Tellers kills the truth.

No one listens to dead men.
The man on the train said,

"Telling the truth is a dangerous
Game if you are the messenger."

TRANSITIONS

The spoons were way too small.
In prison they were all one size.
Big-or as Mama use to call them, tablespoons.

How much time would it take,
For me to forget how it looks or feels,
To hold a small, shallow dinner spoon in my hand?

When I came home from spending
Six-years at the Chillicothe Correctional
Institution for a crime that I didn't commit.

That's the first thing that hit me,
And it knocked me off balance.
The spoons were way too small.

I'd been eating with big, broad and
Wide tablespoons.
Spoons with muscles.

We could just shovel food down the
Chute with a spoon like that.
Mine was a manly-man dining utensil one.

No edible substance could escape.
I tried, I really tried, but my fingers kept dropping
That shallow other thing from my grasp.

Back in the free world now, I mostly eat meat
And Leave my spoon alone.
But anything else is free game,

My spoon can handle it.
I even use it's edges.
As a knife-ain't no dinner spoon can do that.

So if you've got a friend who's been missing
For years and he doesn't want to tell
You where he's been.

Place a "Welcome Home" cake in front of
Him, hove him a big spoon and say,
"Welcome home, Sweetheart. "Here, Cut me a slice."

DEAD MEN WALKING

Black mothers give birth to stillborn sons,
Destined for the Walking Dead.

Black Mother's warn their sons.
"Don't backtalk the police and never ever run
Son, never run."

Black mothers sound like
policemen, yet their warnings are in vain.

Black sons are arrested,
shot, and killed by the hundreds each year.

The Black male is a Dead Man
Walking and deadly force is needed
to stop him.
...any policeman can tell you that.

No matter if young or
old, or in the street in
daylight, with his
hands held up,
or being dragged with a broken back.

Deadly force is needed to stop him.
...any policeman can tell you that.

The black male is a Dead Man Walking.
...any policeman can tell you that.

SMELLS

Smells, that until
My mother died,
Were just a part of me.

Until she died,
I'd never lived
outside of the Ghetto
and never realized,

How trapped I'd been
By the smells of
My own neighborhood.

The wet, rusty smell of
The sewer in the streets,
and The dead, rotten air, of
The car junkyard at the corner,

But nothing could compete
With the smell of piss and
Vomit that filled the

Hallways and alleys
Late at night when the bars closed.

I felt uncomfortable
Walking where those
Familiar smells weren't
Present-White neighborhoods

The sounds were easy to separate,
Loud talking, horns blaring,
Metal doors slamming, police sirens -
Very distinct, unmistakable contrasts

But for me it was the smells
That held the greater contrast

The damp, rusty smell of
sewer pipes, piss and vomit
and rotten stuff of empty lots

My walk to the bus stop
To go to school was accompanied
By the smell of dead rats
In the alley

Or the cheap wine-soaked smell of vomit
Spewed onto the sidewalk
From the belly of a drunk

On the weekends, the choking
smell of piss greeted me in the
hallway After the guys
stopped to take a leak

Those were the smells that separated
Me a world away from the
White world.

Smells that until my mother died
And I was exposed to others

I accepted daily as normal.

THE AMERICAN MYTH

What is a myth?
A lie that has been told by
so many for so long it is
accepted as the truth.

The American myth is
If you cry injustice,
Long enough- Show Black mothers
Crying on IV and

Clog the Streets
With Marchers
Loudly Protesting
Systematic murder,

Something will change.
Nothing has changed,
Except the scope of the Murder.

The thing that Must be changed
Is our evaluation of
The American System

And why it is
Murdering
Its Black citizens.

YOU AIN'T NO HERO
YOU KILL COPS

Rosa Parks brought a nation to its feet
By refusing to get up
And started a movement -
She didn't kill no cops.

Dr. Martin Luther King
Marched, was jailed and died
For America to meet its
Promise - he didn't kill no cops.

But you kill cops.
Whose liberation are you fighting for?
What movement do you represent?

You sabotage protest,
Breed hopelessness,
Dis-credit legitimate pain
And foment fabricated fury.

The only movement
You create is backlash.
Coward.
You kill cops.

Whose neighborhood
Are you protecting?
You kill cops.

You bring the heat down on
Everyone and generate new
Explosions of brutality
From those who beat us.

You kill cops.
You bring pain and
Suffering to everyone you meet.
A coward spewing hatred in the streets.

Leave my neighborhood.
You are a killer,
Poison to all around you
A traitor to any movement.

Get the hell off my
Streets You selfish
Son-of-a-bitch-
You kill cops.

BLACKED OUT

Maybe it's a class thing.
Blue collar worker
Glad to see another black face,
Relieved even.

Looks my way and smiles.
Isn't threatened by my being here.

Professional's,
That's another thing.
Comfortable as the
Only black person in the room,

Gets nervous when I'm near.
Moves away before
we inhabit the same area.

Looks down and
Around so as not to see me.

I didn't come to the party
To keep the Brightness of
Whiteness from shining down
On him alone.

Exposed, he turns away.
Wickedly, I walk toward him,
Fist thrust forward for a bump.

"Good to meet you,
Brother," I say, heartily.

"Nice to meet you too."
He dryly replies.

Denuded by my fist,
he turned quickly away.

I walk away laughing to myself.
His efforts to sever
himself from his Blackness

Crushed by a word
And a fist bump.

UNREALIZED HOMECOMING

Why do I feel empty
Or feel anything at all
For coming home to Africa
For Africa is not my home not anymore.

The others are still treated
As if they were members
Of the royal family that once ruled
This realm because they were white.

Yet I,too, am given the same
Downcast eye and retreating bow
Given my tour mates
I am saddened by it and wonder why.

"We need your money.
My family lives better
Because of the money you bring".

I come to Africa to find my home
And am happy that I have money to share
But am saddened that I have lost my kinship
By your treating me as one of them.

Chapter Two

Spinning

SPINNING

As his world spins
From Colored to Black

Constantly displacing, a quiet
Comfortable, Knowingness,

With Loud, Challenging,
Unapologetic sounds

Unsatisfied, wanting more
(More than before Sounds)

Putting a "Yes sir"
And "No sir" universe
In it's place

Standing up
And standing pat
Without needing
Approval sounds.

Yes, this Black
Thing is alright.

WHO ARE YOU ANYWAY

"Who are you, anyway?"
Said the white guy across
The hall as I topped the stairs.

He wanted to sound tough,
But It sounded like a cry.
He needed to establish some context.

Was I White, Yellow, Blue,
Brown, Or whatever?

He looked at least sixty
And he had to know.
Had to know before he could relax.

What shelf could he place me on?
How should he respond to me
While we lived in such close
quarters temporarily?

My wife and I, white,
were just checking out
Along-term care facility
for the weekend.

One in which he certainly
wouldn't want to stay in
If I were the wrong color.

He spoke again. "What are you? Puerto
Rican Or something?
I looked at him blankly and
Gave no response.

He turned away,
Unsatisfied,
And closed his door.

I stayed in that complex
For three months
while getting treatment
for cancer and never saw my neighbor again.

He was more afraid of me
Than I was of him,
That's one reason
Black men can get shot so easily.

It's a Good thing
I'm not big and dark-skinned.
As some people often tell me,
And I hate it, "You don't look Black"
Well, that's not always a bad thing.

DON'T CURSE ME YOU DON'T LOOK BLACK

Don't tell me,
"You Don't Look Black."
And expect me to love it,
Because it's too painful'

Those sick Blacks in the 50s
Who didn't look Black,
Left their culture,
Even rejected their mothers

To join a culture
That despised them,
Loved to be told,
"You Don't Look Black"

Lena Horne,
One of the best Black
Actresses of the 50's
"Didn't Look Black"

Yet, she never got paid
As much as white actresses
Who weren't as
Qualified as her.

I can remember being told as a kid,
Martin "You don't look Black"
The usher at the RKO
Theater didn't seem to care,

I still had to sit in the
Balcony If I wanted to get in.

One summer when taking
A family trip from Cincinnati to Selma,
We stopped at a gas
Station in Kentucky,

I stepped out of the backseat
And headed toward the bathroom,
The owner ran out of the office
And shouted,

"Not in my bathroom, you ain't"
Maybe it was our Ohio License
Plates Because as people always
Told me, Martin, "You don't look Black."

WORD PLAY

The N-Word
Isn't as
Destructive As the
F-Word.

Don't get caught up
By the sleight-of-hand
When bigots
Proclaim,

The N-Word
Is a Disgraceful
Discriminating
And Prejudicial Attack.

Some define the
N-Word By its color.
If that's so
I was born an N-Word.

But I am not defined
By that terrible
F-Word,
Thank you, Jesus.

Society flashes the
N-Word
Like Three-Card-Monte
Buries the hated F-Word

At the bottom
Of the deck
Concealed by
The flurry.

A coat of many colors
The N-Word is used
Inject In anger,
Even in admiration:

"Joe Louis, now, that Nigger
was bad." The N-Word is here to stay.
No one was born with the F-Word.
It's that damn F-Word that will kill you.

FAILURE-run from it!
Failure will suffocate your soul.

ONLY IN WHITE AMERICA

Affluenza;
Virus which affects victims
Of affluent parents
Who never set limits.

In a drunken
While driving without a license
He crashed head-on into another car,
Killing four people.

"A victim of Affluenza,
Parents never dared set limits
On his behavior,"
His expensive attorney argued.

"Nannies and teachers
Did not dare refuse his demands".
"How can he be
Held responsible now?"

"Innocent by virtue of his affluent
Upbringing," the jury declared.
I never figured it was an illness
Or a negative condition.

It seemed to be a privilege to someone like me,
To be able to do whatever he wanted,
And never worry about how much it might
Cost, or how it might harm someone else.

As a Black man who would be imprisoned
For such an act.
His White privilege may have kept him free
From being imprisoned By the state,

But without the influence of affluenza
What would he do behind bars?
I know the answer to that question.
He'd be lucky to survive.

"A victim of affluenza' his expensive
Attorney argued."
His parents never dared
Set limits on his behavior.

But what can I, a Black Man, do
With his affluence and my influence in this
Society? Not nearly as much as a white man
With the same Affluence.

Sadly, the class system
That we've all heard since grade School
Doesn't exist in America is still alive
And stronger than racism.

It is not as hopeless as it sounds.
That means that
Racism can be beaten
And the real beast is Class.

UNDERCOVER

Dear Cousin Jim,

After all these years
I've finally made it.

It was tough during the 60's,
Didn't think I'd survive.

Never thought I'd
Come out whole, Jim, But here I am.

Had to change my
Game And move to the suburbs
(Control Blockbusting)

Denounced the KKK
(Joined The Auxiliary Police)

Wore a Suit and Tie
(Became The Loan Officer at The Bank)

Joined The Controlling Political Party
(Kept wealthy school districts apart from
those others)

Your disguise worked, Jim.
After all these years
I'm still alive,
Still riding high through the land,
Even got some new Klan going.

Yep, they ain't got rid of me yet, cousin
Jim. They ain't got rid of meyet.

Yours truly,

James Crowe

SQUARING UP

The ninth floor of Wall Street
in New York City
Is a great location for anyone
Enthralled by the city's storied reputation.

From my window the Brooklyn Bridge
Seems close enough to touch
And even with the windows closed,
The sounds of New York Climb the nine stories.

I enjoy working in lower Manhattan
Taking the long island railroad
Into the City and hopping the subway
Down to Wall Street.

The walk past the Stock Exchange
Always gives me a rush
And propels me to my office
Where I become part of the city

As the Northeast Director
Of Major Gifts For the United Negro College Fund.
I am a specialist at raising large sums of money
For higher education.

In Mama's words,
I am good at helping others
do the best they can.

Carrying a leather briefcase
and wearing a Brooks Brothers suit,
I look nothing like Mama
would have remembered.

The guys back on Gest Street
would sneer At my Wall Street costume
and say I've "squared up."

Maybe I have become a square.
...it beats the hell out of going to prison.

UNEASY FEELING

It is not easy for a man whose forefathers were
slaves to act as a master over others.

Why do I feel guilty
For coming home to africa,
For Africa is not my home,
Not anymore.

In Cape Town
I feel a part
Being served by Africans
While dining in my 5-star hotel.

Coming Home:

Robben Island/Mandela's Prison Cell
27 years building a nation
Molding South Africa into one.

It is not easy for a man whose forefathers were
slaves to act a sa master over others.

In Johannesburg on safari
With my African guide
I'm the great white hunter
With a black face.

Coming Home:

Soweto Township/Sharpesville
Massacre Mandela & Bishop Tutu's homes
Two Nobel Prize winners
On the same street.

Apartheid Museum/so many divisions
Based on color

And so many laws to prop them up
"almost like your American Apartheid,"
Says a Brit, calling it for what it is.

Stopping for biscuits and tea
While on Safari as the black bwana,
And moving on looking for Leopard
Following the guide following his tracks.

It is not easy for a man whose forefathers were
slaves to act as a master over others.

Coming Home:

Huntington Village/tourist attraction
40,000 homes, no running water,
TV aerials in view.

We exit our bus and I stand there the sole
Black man in our group as a group
Of black kids all under the age of ten
Run out to meet us.

A southern belle of good intentions
Brings a box of candy to pass out to them.
The kids love it. I hate it.

It is like feeding the animals
And I am part of the group
That is feeding them.

One boy, smaller than the others,
Ignores the candy, and runs to me,
Clings to my leg, and looks up adoringly
With eyes like mine.

I love him instantly
And find redemption in his grasp.

My guide lives in this village
Of concrete blocks
And works every six weeks
At the hotel with two weeks off without pay.
But he is happy that I am here.

Tourism pays the bills.
And I finally understand
That to him and other Africans
I was an American tourist first
And an African American second, if at all.

IT AIN'T WHAT IT SEEMS

Up top is always best
Don't you agree,
The best seats are always
In the balcony.

The top prices
For theater tickets
Are always those seats
Above the floor.

If I were a member of the KKK
And couldn't sit in the balcony
Of the Movie Theater
Downtown.

I'd be pissed,
Watching all those Blacks
Being **forced**
To sit in the balcony.

And take the best seats
At the Movie Theater...
Theater Downtown.

Segregation is hell.
Who came up with this shit?

I DON'T EAT 'EM

It took me awhile
Before I could quite comprehend
What Southerners' meant
With the sign,

"We don't serve Coloreds"

I grew up eating colards
So I figured they weren't
Talking about greens,
After all what Southern
Cafe wouldn't serve Collards?

My stepdaddy who's from
The South, said the sign
Means they don't serve
Colored People.

But what if I'm hungry
And ready to eat,
Can't I eat there?
Not if You're Colored,
You know that.

Don't start being
A smart-ass,
Don't start any
Of that Black shit.

I couldn't help myself,
After a few minutes, I saw the
Sign. Before Daddy's
Outstretched arms Could stop me,

I stepped toward the cafe,
Opened the door
Walked right in, and before the
Startled waitress could Faint, I said,

"A full slab of ribs, please, and two
Pepsis to go. I don't eat Coloreds."

CITY LIFE

He is a night stalker
Who warms himself in bars
Until closing time
And then

Leases a stool
At the nearest White Castle
Until dawn

He calls tramps
By their first name

And huddles
Around their barrel fires
In vacant lots
Waiting for the sun to rise

Sometimes he falls asleep
On a bench in Washington
Park, With nothing more than
The night to cover him

But even there
No one tries to harm him

He lives in a sea of parasites
Rubbing shoulders with
Every Predator and jackal of
The Lowest kind

Yet, somehow. He survives.
He has to.
He's homeless.

WHEN THE NOISE STOPS

White noise is there
But not there,
It is ever present
But not everywhere.

Barely noticeable.
Easy to ignore.

It's a wall of sound,
Porous, soft and relaxing,
Yet acts as a stabilizer.
A foundation for creating.

If noise is truly on
A spectrum like colors,
Then what is black noise?

Black noise is out there,
But not where anyone
Pays any attention.
Barely noticeable.

Easy to ignore
While riding around it on the
Through it on the expressway
Or under it on the subway.

Black noise is uncomfortable.
Uneasy, raucous.
Palpable but untouchable.
An angry carrousel of sound.

Geographically smothered
It's the only noise

That can be seen
as well as heard.

What happens
when the noise stops?
Meanacing, Explosive, Silence.
Be thankful for the noise.

DON'T DRINK COFFEE

Don't drink coffee
Daddy warned me,
"It'll make you black."

I drank lots of milk
And It never
Made me white.

He was warning me
That anyone in America
Not White was Black.
And that was bad.

No matter what his color,
Muslim, Asian, Indian
Puerto Rican, or Jew.

In the U.S.,
White is the only color
That matters,

Thank you.

To stay alive,
Daddy said,
Don't drink coffee
It'll make youBlack.

NORTH CAROLINA CLOUDS

Slaves picked cotton
In North Carolina
That was so pristine
Some called the cotton clouds.

But the cotton was not clouds.
The cotton was anchored to land,
It pricked fingers
And drew blood.

The clouds exploded
Like white canon shot
In blue North Carolina skies.

North Carolina Clouds
Are an artist's delight.
They explode with a soft whiteness
That changes quietly by the second.

North Carolina Clouds
Are screechingly high one moment,
And, yet, so low the next
Your breath is smothered.

North Carolina Clouds are fickle.
I've seen them burst into glee
While playing peek-a-boo

With the sun and ferociously
Blacken before dumping torrents
Of rain on me as I stood at
The bus stop on my wayto........
It doesn't really matter.

Slaves picked cotton
Under North Carolina
Clouds that still prick fingers
And draw black Carolina blood.

THINNING OUT

The earth wakes and shakes again
Breaking, remaking, molding
And scolding man
As it forms and reforms.

Imploding, folding, boiling
Magma claims its molten
Dominion over man by cremating
A Hilton Hotel or an Island.

"Man was given
Dominion over the earth",
says the myth.
But no one told Mother Earth

That, or if they did
She didn't believe it.
She thunders and frolics
In her swimming hole the sea

Swallowed the Sargasso,
Hiccupped the Pacific, and
Tsunamied nations on a whim.

Newscasters call each loss
A disaster.
Mother Earth calls it
Thinning out.
Nature's guilty little pleasure.

HARD CONCRETE TO GREEN GRASS

My sisters drew chalk lines,
Played four-square with a soccer ball
And laughed on the concrete sidewalk
In front of our apartment.

Ace, Bop, Milt, and Me
Threw craps against the concrete deck
Between the garbage cans
Hiding the game in the alley.

Grass tried to grow
Between the cobblestone bricks
But the buildings were too close
And the sun lost the war.

Little light could get through
And the bricks were too moist and dark.
We knew what our world offered
And learned how to enjoy its pleasures.

We enjoyed our play
In our concrete world
And except for every July 4th
When Daddy took us away,
Expected nothing more.

Our concrete world faded
On July 4th each year
When Daddy took us
into the rolling hills and green meadows
Of Winton Woods.

It was fun and wild.
We ran around without shoes
On and didn't worry about nails
And brokens glass.

Played softball under the trees
And we all ate barbecue
From the grill before we left.

The ride home was quiet,
Unlike the excited one on the way up.
My sisters sat back
On the seat and slept
while I looked out the window.

When we got back home
I jumped out of the car
To run and find Milt
Or, Bop, and the girls went inside
All talking about the trip.

I enjoyed Winton Woods
But it was good
To be back on the block.

GROWN-UP GAMES

Growing up we played games
By grown-up rules,
Four-square, hit the ball
On the line - its out.

Simon says,
Say it like Simon or you lose.
I wish I could play grown-up games
By growing up rules.

Move into a new neighborhood
Make friends with your neighbor
Get invited to his house you're in
By growing up rules

Made friends with my neighbor
got invited to his house
Got in but I lost.
I hadn't learned how to play
Grown up games by grown up rules

After dinner, my neighbor asked,
"Going to Cannes this year-to the Festival?"
"No, I don't think I will." I replied.
"Why, don't you like Cannes?"

Not knowing how to play grown-up games
Instead of lying and saying,
Yes, but I'm tied up.

I said, "No, it's boring
During the Festival
too many celebrity seekers."

I made the wrong move,
Trying to play a grown-up game
Using grown-up rules.

I lost playing the grown-up game
And never heard from that neighbor again.

THE GHETTO

When Huey Newton came to Cincinnati
He said we lived in the Ghetto
And would die in the Ghetto
Unless we changed it.

Elvis Pressley's song "In the Ghetto"
Told the story of a Black child
Born to a Ghetto mother
Who didn't need another mouth to feed

Who is Eventually killed while stealing a car.
I never have gotten used
To the Inner City Charade
It's more propaganda than situational.

Kind of like when the slaves
Were declared free after the Civil War
And still treated as slaves
All the way through Jim Crow.

As a teen-ager, living in the Ghetto,
Unlike the adults,
I didn't yearn for it
to be something else.

I felt safe in my neighborhood
Away from white folk.
I know who liked me, who disliked me,
And most importantly,
Who to stay away from
To keep from being hurt.

Out of the Ghetto
I didn't know who to avoid.

Who might hurt me,
Who would help me?

And I didn't know where to run
If someone was after me.
In the Ghetto not only did I know
Every ally and street with my eyes closed,

I knew which doors would open
When I knocked.
The Ghetto stood
For something.

What's in a name?
If that name is the Ghetto,
It is where you live.
It could bring comfort or explode with fury.

If you were from the Ghetto
You had an identify, you were a force.
History revealed that my Ghetto safety was a vision.
I felt safe but I was riding a false tide
Of security in a boat programmed to sink.

The Inner City emasculated the Ghetto
And watered down its identity.
My safety may have been only a vision
But just being young and ignorant

I was free to walk through my neighborhood
Without fear day or night.

My greatest fear was getting caught
Coming up the fire
Escape to our 4th floor apartment
After my 11 pm curfew.

Chapter Three

Being There

GEST STREET

Living on Gest Street
Generally meant learning
To go with the flow
And Staying above it.

People passing through
Always wanted something.
Some, like Ed, wanted only
To buy girls.

I knew right away
What he wanted
And it wasn't,
"Someone nice and clean."

"You know what I mean,"
He continued.
"I'll give you twenty dollars'
If you can do that for me."

"Think you can find one?"
He asked as if ordering steak.

This wasn't the first time
I'd been stopped by Ed
Cruising the neighborhood in his car
Looking for girls.

He always wanted the same thing,
"A nice clean colored girl,
To have fun with."

I took his money.
He parked near the alley
So that I could bring
Someone to him.

When I peered from
Around the corner of
The alley about 30 minutes
Later, Ed's car was gone.

He never learned.
Ed risked losing his money
Or worse, each time he came.

Yet, he always came back,
Same time, same station.

HALF A PAIR

One lone sock
Without the other
Seems as useless
As half a pair.

Fairly useful
As a glove,
A polishing cloth,
A catcher's mitt.

I once used it
As a stopper
To take a bath with-

Though admittedly
The bath was very short.
This sock is better old
Than when new

When new it was strong
and stiff strangling,
choking my calf
Leaving indentations on my skin.

But now it caresses my leg
Softly, like a lover
Gently and with glee
If a sock could be gleeful.

One lone sock caressing
One leg seems useful
Enough to me,
For one lone leg is all I've got.

THE NUMBERS GAME

When I was 10years old
My mother would give me 50 cents
And would send me across the hall
Once a week to Miss Louise,

The Numbers Lady.
I'd give her the slip of paper
That my Mother had given me
With the number written on it.

Miss Louise would open the paper,
Look at it, and drop it
Into a bell jar
Next to her door.

She'd tell me to say "Hi,"
To my Mother
And close the door.
When my Mother "Hit the Number"

She would give part of it
To Miss Louise
And Miss Louise
Would give part of it to me.

Miss Louise, now she knew what
The Numbers Game was all about.
That's the kind of numbers game
That I want to play.

BROTHERHOOD

I knew they weren't my Mama's Children.
Three boys: Tee, Woody, and Joseph,
None of them looked like me.
Plus, they were Daddy's kids

And Daddy was my Step-Dad.
But my four sisters and brother didn't know it,
Because I was already there
Before they were born.

My four sisters and four brothers all
Had the same father.
My four sisters, one brother, and I
All had the same mom.

It seems that Daddy was the winner,
He had eight and Mama had just me.
Daddy also had two more sons and two more
Girls; Louie Junior, Big Joe, Eleanora, and Shirley.

And I've met them all.
They are all my brothers and sisters,
And I am their brother.

I believe that all families are like mine.
We are all brothers and sisters,
Regardless of parents.
No step, no half, we are all one.

If 23 & Me would go back far enough
I bet that's what they would find...
After all our links crossed
And crisscrossed, that we are all one.
One Big Family.

THE JUNKMAN

Navigator Jack
Made most things sound easy

Unshaven, wearing dark pants and shoes
With lots of space at the toes.

He looked like a bum in his outfit
But didn't act like one

Anything you asked him
To do He could do it

If you looked into his eyes
Like I did

You could see the true
Navigator

Looked straight into your heart
When he talked

Nobody but him would know
What you talked about

The Navigator Jack
I saw behind those eyes

Could be anything he wanted,
And at that moment he wanted to be our Junkman.

NO APOLOGIES

Poverty lives in their clothes
Settles in their school lunch bags

Rustles in their holey drawers
Shows itself at play

They don't make excuses
For their poverty

Beat the hell out of anyone
Who finds their situation funny.

They aren't proud
Of being poor,

And aren't about to let others
Make them feel Ashamed of who they are

The Pressley girls
Make no apologies.

OLD WORDS

When I go to my old neighborhood
Or talk to my sisters.
Old words like old friends
Find their way to my tongue
And tumble freely from my lips.

Old words that have been hidden
Away banished in a timelock,
Words of little schooling,
Warm words, ticklish under-the-cover
Words spoken in childish joy.

Old words dipped in Xmas jollies
Seasoned with Thanksgiving
Laughter at the kid's table,
Syrup-like, sticky, pulling me
Home again in forgotten sweetness.

Old words,
Words are never forgotten
But quickly remembered
Whenever that touchstone is near.

BAITS

I've spent my whole life
Dealing with baits.

Take these minnows for instance
Like my first wife
They're short, skinny, and not too curvy.
But can they entice something big?
You better believe it.

Unlike traps
Baits have to be seen to work.
Any fool can fall into a trap.
It don't take no fool to take the bait.

Just look at these crawdads.
I ain't found nothing yet
Won't snap at a crawdad.
Shit, you can even catch people
With 'em if you had a mind to.

Bait depends on two things though.
Who are you trying to catch
And how much time
You got to catch 'em.
You know what?

I hooked a New York City stockbroker
With a 9-lb barrel of crawdads.
The fool thought they were lobsters.
Baits ain't always physical either.
Some are in the mind.

I've seen people fool themselves,
Chasing bait they knew was false.

Foolishness some people call it.
Others call it hope.
Well, I've got to go now.

Got to go home, greet my son.
Said he'd come home
Tonight if I just sent the fare.
I wired the money to Western Union.
I've spent my whole life dealing with baits

ANOTHER INOCULATION

He grew up believing he was healthy
And why not?
He'd never been outside of the Ghetto
Where it was bad to be Black.

One day his parents took him aside
And told him that his Blackness was an
Illness to the general society,
He must be Inoculated to survive in it.

So they dressed him up in his Sunday Best
And sent him Uptown to be Inoculated.

And everywhere he went,
In every store he stopped,
Wherever he touched merchandise,
Walked aimlessly about,
Or looked at items a bit too long

Someone shadowed his every move.
Disapproving stares challenged his every step.
Security staff were on high alert,
And counter staff spat bitterly,
"What do you want Boy?!

He was hurt and ashamed
Of being unable to shop anywhere
Without Having to think
About touching Merchandise,
Looking at items hungrily,
Or staying in a dressing room too long.

From now on he must always be
Aware of how his Blackness

Affected others, And learn to live
With how it affected him.

He turned slowly andlowered his head,
Took one step forward,
And didn't stop until he was home.
Another Inoculation complete.

MY BEAUTIFUL FLOWER

A flower is noted
For its beauty,
For its scent,
Not necessarily
For its strength.

It is full of light,
Shining brightly,
Like a diamond
Under the sun.

Its beauty
Is cradled by the stern,
Its source of both
Strength and weakness.

The stem may crumple,
split apart,
Totally lose its strength
And be unable to support
The flower as before.

The flower
Must find a new means
To stay afloat,
To grow, to stay alive,
Or to die.

So it was with my beautiful flower.
Her stem was split in two.
As many black stems

Have been split apart
From their flowers in America.

The male half
Of My Beautiful Flower's stem
Was sent to a prison
To get crushed.

Bruised, and torn,
The female half
Was left to hold the flower
aloft alone.

Yet, the flower survived
And grew to be stronger
And more beautiful
Than before.

And ever since then
My Beautiful Flower
Has been struggling
To bring the full light
Of freedom and liberty

To those flowers
Whose stems
Have been hacked off
Through, poverty, prison,
And injustice.

She continues to demonstrate
Through her own growth
That the mutilation
Of a Black stem

Does not negate its recovery
And its ability
To contribute to the continued
Growth and beauty
Of a Beautiful Flower.

Happy Birthday, Ayanna

Soyini Love, Dad

Never Give Up The Struggle/My Beautiful
Flower - You Are Winning

IT'S ONLY A PURSE

It was shaped like a mail pouch
And carved like a Mexican saddle
It had a slim shoulder strap
That could be worn or taken off.

But what impressed me most
And My mama too,
Was her name "Carrie" carved
In red and green letters on the flap.

She told me it was a handmade purse
Made by my real father,
Big Red, while he was in prison
And except for me

It was the only thing
She'd gotten from him
And she wasn't sure
If she wanted to keep it.

"Why didn't you tell me
Anything about my Father before ?" I said.
"Go ask Mr. Earl over at the Cleaners on 5th Street,"
She said, "He'll tell you about your Father."

"He'll tell you about Big Red."
"He was handsome, tall and light-skinned.
Always dressed the best," said Mr. Earl,
"I kept his clothes sharp."

"All the girls liked him and he liked them.
He liked you too.
Said you were his favorite.
He was unfaithful and your Mama left him".

Got in a fight with a man downtown,
Knocked him down,
The man's head hit the sidewalk,
Killing him. Red got his twenty years.

I don't know if Mama threw the purse away
But I never saw it again
And I never saw Big Red
It was probably good Mama left him when she did

I didn't need a father,
I had my stepdad and I had her
Anyway, I would have kept the purse.
It was handmade and had her name carved into it.

THERE WAS A NAME FOR IT

It was a kind of baseball.
We called it Strike Out
We played it in the vacant lot
Between my apartment and Jim's

We'd break a piece of brick
And draw an oblong box
On the wall of my building
Because the ground was flatter there.

A box that resembled
A batting cage,
About as wide as my shoulders
And as deep as my knees

Then we'd throw a softball, tennis,
Or a rubber ball,
Into the box and try
To strike the batter out.

I learned to play Strike Out
Before I stepped on a Baseball field
Maybe that's why
I didn't make a good outfielder

But I could hit any pitch
No matter where
In the strike zone
They threw it.

THE ROLLAWAY BED

My rollaway bed was
Quite a contraption.
It had one hard mattress
That folded up like a biscuit.

The springs became the borders
On each side
To hold the mattress in.

The steel footers folded up
Against the springs
And Freed the wheels to roam.

My rollaway bed
Slept in a kitchen closet
In the daytime
Away from the rats and mice
That sometimes tried to eat
It's Cotton filling.

At night, it lay unfolded in
The Kitchen as my raft upon
A green linoleum sea.

I kept the kitchen light on
Until I was completely
Undressed, because the
Moment that I yanked
The light off,
The rats would come poking
And Peeking out of the walls.

I didn't care about the ones
Scraping the sink.
They were too faraway
To leap into bed with me.

It was the ones whose nails were razoring
Across the floor that set off my alarms.

I slept with my gym shoes in the bed.
One shoe under each arm like a
torpedo.

For our whole two years on 8th street,
I slept ready to fire at the slightest whimper.
I never threw my shoe until a rat was almost
Touching my bed and I was sure
To hit or kill him.

And not once did a rat stay on my bed
And I never got bitten.
I learned that rat warfare is best for late
night

So that you can nap peacefully before the
sun comes up and then fold up your
rollaway bed.

HAVING MY OWN BIKE

I'd always wanted a bike.
Having my own bike
Would put wings on my feet.

With my bike,
A patched-up, blue, twenty-six-inch
Huffy with a custom RollFast seat,
And two mismatched fenders

I could leave
13th St. behind
And for awhile
Forget having to return.

I could race
To Eden Park
And back with my own bike
Or just ride there

By myself and not worry
About making it home before dark
If I wanted to earn extra money
I could put a basket
On the handlebars,
A carrier on the rear fender
And I'd be ready to carry groceries
Home from Kroger's for tips

Having my own bike
Meant Much more than just riding.

Having my own bike
Meant having the freedom
To go where I wanted to be.
Without asking permission.
There was nothing else like it...

SHEDDING MY SKIN

I loved the Ghetto
Living there made a statement
The Ghetto was part of me
I felt safe in the Ghetto.

Daddy got a better job
We moved out of the Ghetto
To a small suburb north,
Of the city

Everyday people walked around
Doing what to them were everyday things.
Walking in and out of neighbor's homes
Stopping and talking in small shops Downtown.

Madeira kids were different from West End kids.
They didn't seem to be afraid
of adults Or of Each other.
They laughed more.
Even in the cold.

What held most clings to me still.
Everyone was clean.
Their clothes looked as if they had just put
them on that morning.

On Gest Street we sometimes wore the same pants
For an entire week.
The streets, the yards, the buildings,
Everywhere I looked.

I found clean. Maybe we moved too quickly.
I felt something like the startled awe
That the blind experience
With the sudden intensity of light.

Maybe people normally
Looked and dressed like them.
Maybe the ones I'd grown with
Were abnormal.

People looked as if they took baths
Every day and sometimes two.
They didn't worry about
Paying the water bill didn't bathe

In number ten-tubs with hot water
Brought in from the sink.
Even before we got into
Our new place, I knew I wanted to live that way.